EMMANUEL JOSEPH

The Classroom of the Cosmos, Gaming, Learning, and the Search for Meaning

Copyright © 2025 by Emmanuel Joseph

All rights reserved. No part of this publication may be reproduced, stored or transmitted in any form or by any means, electronic, mechanical, photocopying, recording, scanning, or otherwise without written permission from the publisher. It is illegal to copy this book, post it to a website, or distribute it by any other means without permission.

First edition

This book was professionally typeset on Reedsy.
Find out more at reedsy.com

Contents

1. Chapter 1 — 1
2. Chapter 2: Gaming as a Gateway to Knowledge — 3
3. Chapter 3: The Science of Play — 5
4. Chapter 4: Virtual Reality: A New Dimension of Learning — 7
5. Chapter 5: The Intersection of Gaming and Education — 9
6. Chapter 6: The Role of Storytelling in Learning — 11
7. Chapter 7: Learning Through Collaboration — 13
8. Chapter 8: Personalized Learning in the Digital Age — 15
9. Chapter 9: The Ethics of Educational Technology — 17
10. Chapter 10: The Future of Learning — 19
11. Chapter 11: The Search for Meaning — 21
12. Chapter 12: Embracing the Infinite Possibilities — 23
13. Chapter 13: Gamification Beyond the Classroom — 25
14. Chapter 14: Cultivating a Growth Mindset — 27
15. Chapter 15: The Power of Reflection — 29

1

Chapter 1

apter 1: The Cosmic Classroom

In a world where education often feels confined to the four walls of a classroom, the concept of learning is evolving. The Cosmic Classroom represents the boundless opportunities for knowledge that exist beyond traditional educational settings. This new classroom is as vast as the universe itself, encompassing everything from video games to virtual reality, and beyond. In this chapter, we explore how the boundaries of learning are being expanded by innovative technologies and unconventional methods, allowing students to explore, discover, and learn in ways that were once unimaginable.

Gaming has emerged as a powerful tool for education, transforming the way students engage with complex subjects. In the Cosmic Classroom, games are not just a form of entertainment, but a means of exploring intricate concepts and developing critical thinking skills. Students can embark on quests that require them to solve puzzles, strategize, and collaborate with peers, all while absorbing knowledge in an interactive and immersive environment. This chapter delves into the various ways gaming is being integrated into educational curriculums, highlighting the benefits and challenges of this approach.

As we venture further into the Cosmic Classroom, we encounter the role of virtual reality in education. Virtual reality (VR) offers students the opportunity to step into entirely new worlds, experiencing history, science, and art in ways that textbooks cannot. In this chapter, we examine the impact of VR on student engagement and retention, as well as its potential to democratize education by providing access to high-quality learning experiences regardless of geographic location. The Cosmic Classroom is a space where imagination and innovation converge, creating endless possibilities for exploration and discovery.

Ultimately, the Cosmic Classroom is about more than just technology; it is about fostering a love of learning that transcends traditional boundaries. By embracing new methods and tools, we can create an educational environment that inspires curiosity and encourages students to pursue their passions. This chapter sets the stage for the journey ahead, inviting readers to join us as we explore the intersection of gaming, learning, and the search for meaning in the universe.

2

Chapter 2: Gaming as a Gateway to Knowledge

Gaming has long been viewed as a pastime, but its potential as an educational tool is gaining recognition. In this chapter, we explore how games can serve as a gateway to knowledge, providing students with engaging and interactive experiences that enhance their understanding of complex subjects. From mathematics to history, games have the power to transform the way we learn, making education more accessible and enjoyable for students of all ages.

One of the key benefits of gaming in education is its ability to make learning fun. Traditional methods of teaching can sometimes feel dry and uninspiring, but games have the power to capture students' attention and keep them engaged. In this chapter, we discuss the various ways that games are being used to teach subjects like math and science, highlighting the advantages of using game-based learning to promote student motivation and enthusiasm.

Games also offer the opportunity for students to develop important skills that go beyond academic knowledge. Critical thinking, problem-solving, and collaboration are just a few of the skills that can be honed through gaming. In this chapter, we examine how games can help students build these essential skills, preparing them for success in both their academic and personal lives. The immersive nature of games allows students to experience challenges and setbacks in a safe environment, fostering resilience and perseverance.

Finally, we consider the potential of gaming to bridge the gap between different learning styles and abilities. Not all students learn in the same way, and games offer a versatile and adaptable approach to education that can accommodate diverse needs. In this chapter, we explore how games can be used to support students with different learning preferences, ensuring that everyone has the opportunity to succeed in the Cosmic Classroom.

3

Chapter 3: The Science of Play

Play is an essential part of human development, and its importance extends far beyond childhood. In this chapter, we delve into the science of play and its role in learning and growth. From cognitive development to emotional well-being, play has a profound impact on our ability to learn and adapt. By understanding the science behind play, we can harness its potential to create more effective and engaging educational experiences.

Research has shown that play is crucial for cognitive development, particularly in young children. Through play, children learn to explore their environment, develop problem-solving skills, and build social connections. In this chapter, we examine the various ways that play contributes to cognitive growth, drawing on insights from developmental psychology and neuroscience. By incorporating elements of play into the Cosmic Classroom, we can create learning experiences that are both enjoyable and effective.

Emotional well-being is another important aspect of play. Play provides a safe space for individuals to express themselves, manage stress, and build resilience. In this chapter, we explore the emotional benefits of play and its role in promoting mental health. By creating a playful and supportive learning environment, we can help students develop the emotional skills they need to thrive in both their academic and personal lives.

Play also fosters creativity and innovation. When we engage in play, we are free to experiment, take risks, and think outside the box. In this chapter, we discuss the ways that play can inspire creativity and drive innovation, both in and out of the classroom. By encouraging a playful mindset, we can empower students to approach challenges with curiosity and confidence.

Ultimately, the science of play reveals that learning and play are not mutually exclusive, but rather complementary. By embracing the principles of play, we can create educational experiences that are both meaningful and enjoyable. This chapter highlights the importance of play in the Cosmic Classroom and sets the stage for a deeper exploration of its potential.

4

Chapter 4: Virtual Reality: A New Dimension of Learning

Virtual reality (VR) is revolutionizing the way we experience the world, and its potential as an educational tool is vast. In this chapter, we explore how VR is transforming the learning landscape, offering students immersive and interactive experiences that bring complex concepts to life. From virtual field trips to 3D visualizations, VR is opening up new dimensions of learning that were once the stuff of science fiction.

One of the most exciting applications of VR in education is the ability to take students on virtual field trips. With VR, students can explore historical sites, visit distant planets, and dive into the depths of the ocean, all from the comfort of their classroom. In this chapter, we discuss the impact of virtual field trips on student engagement and understanding, highlighting the ways that VR can make learning more tangible and memorable.

VR also offers powerful tools for visualizing complex concepts. In subjects like science and mathematics, understanding abstract ideas can be challenging. VR allows students to interact with 3D models and simulations, making it easier to grasp difficult concepts. In this chapter, we examine how VR is being used to enhance learning in STEM fields, providing students with a deeper and more intuitive understanding of the material.

Accessibility is another important consideration in the Cosmic Classroom, and VR has the potential to democratize education by providing high-quality learning experiences to students regardless of their location. In this chapter, we explore how VR can bridge the gap between different learning environments, ensuring that all students have access to the resources they need to succeed.

Finally, we consider the future of VR in education and the possibilities it holds for the next generation of learners. As technology continues to advance, the potential for VR to transform education is only growing. This chapter invites readers to imagine the possibilities and consider how we can harness the power of VR to create a more inclusive and engaging educational landscape.

5

Chapter 5: The Intersection of Gaming and Education

The intersection of gaming and education is a dynamic and evolving field, with the potential to reshape the way we approach teaching and learning. In this chapter, we explore the ways that gaming and education intersect, highlighting the benefits and challenges of integrating game-based learning into the classroom. From educational games to gamified learning environments, the possibilities are endless.

Educational games are one of the most direct ways that gaming intersects with education. These games are designed with specific learning objectives in mind, providing students with a fun and engaging way to practice and reinforce their skills. In this chapter, we discuss the various types of educational games available, from math and science games to language and literacy games. We also examine the impact of these games on student motivation and achievement, highlighting the potential for games to make learning more enjoyable and effective.

Gamified learning environments take the principles of gaming and apply them to the broader educational context. This approach involves incorporating elements of game design, such as points, levels, and challenges, into the classroom. In this chapter, we explore how gamification can enhance student engagement and motivation, creating a more interactive and dynamic learning experience. We also discuss the potential challenges of gamification, such as ensuring that the focus remains on learning rather than competition.

The intersection of gaming and education also extends to the development of digital literacy skills. In today's digital age, it is essential for students to be proficient in using technology, and gaming can provide a valuable platform for developing these skills. In this chapter, we consider how gaming can help students build digital literacy, from navigating online environments to coding and programming.

Ultimately, the intersection of gaming and education represents an exciting frontier for the future of learning. By embracing the potential of games, we can create educational experiences that are both engaging and effective. This chapter invites readers to explore the possibilities and consider how we can harness the power of gaming to enhance education in the Cosmic Classroom.

6

Chapter 6: The Role of Storytelling in Learning

Storytelling has been a fundamental part of human culture for thousands of years, and its power to educate and inspire is still relevant today. In this chapter, we explore the role of storytelling in learning, highlighting the ways that stories can be used to convey complex ideas and engage students in meaningful ways. From traditional narratives to interactive storytelling, the Cosmic Classroom is a space where stories come to life.

One of the key benefits of storytelling is its ability to make abstract concepts more relatable and understandable. When we hear a story, we can visualize the events, empathize with the characters, and grasp the underlying messages. In this chapter, we explore how storytelling can be used to teach complex subjects, from history to science, in a way that resonates with students. By incorporating storytelling into the Cosmic Classroom, we can create a more engaging and memorable learning experience.

Interactive storytelling is another powerful tool for education. Unlike traditional narratives, interactive stories allow students to make choices and influence the outcome of the story. This participatory approach encourages critical thinking and problem-solving, as students must consider the consequences of their decisions. In this chapter, we examine the various ways that interactive storytelling is being used in education, from choose-your-own-adventure books to digital platforms that allow for real-time decision-making.

Storytelling also has the power to foster empathy and cultural awareness. By sharing stories from diverse perspectives, we can help students develop a deeper understanding of different cultures and experiences. In this chapter, we discuss the importance of diverse narratives in the Cosmic Classroom and the role of storytelling in promoting inclusivity and empathy. By exposing students to a wide range of stories, we can encourage them to think critically about their own beliefs and values.

Ultimately, storytelling is a timeless and versatile tool that can enrich the learning experience in countless ways. Whether through traditional narratives, interactive stories, or diverse perspectives, storytelling has the power to captivate, educate, and inspire. This chapter highlights the enduring relevance of storytelling in the Cosmic Classroom and invites readers to consider how they can incorporate stories into their own educational practices.

7

Chapter 7: Learning Through Collaboration

Collaboration is a cornerstone of effective learning, and the Cosmic Classroom is no exception. In this chapter, we explore the importance of collaborative learning and the ways that it can be fostered through gaming and technology. By working together, students can develop critical social skills, build meaningful connections, and achieve a deeper understanding of the material.

One of the key benefits of collaborative learning is the opportunity for peer-to-peer interaction. When students work together, they can share ideas, challenge each other's thinking, and provide support and encouragement. In this chapter, we examine the various ways that collaborative learning can be facilitated, from group projects to online discussion forums. By creating a collaborative learning environment, we can help students develop the skills they need to succeed in both academic and professional settings.

Gaming offers unique opportunities for collaboration, as many games require players to work together to achieve a common goal. In this chapter, we explore how cooperative gaming can enhance learning, promoting teamwork, communication, and problem-solving. We discuss the benefits of multiplayer games and the ways that they can be integrated into the classroom to create a more interactive and dynamic learning experience.

Technology also plays a crucial role in facilitating collaboration. Digital tools and platforms can connect students from different locations, allowing them to collaborate on projects and share their work with a wider audience. In this chapter, we examine the impact of technology on collaborative learning and the ways that it can be used to enhance student engagement and participation. By leveraging technology, we can create a more connected and inclusive educational environment.

Ultimately, collaboration is about more than just working together; it is about building a sense of community and shared purpose. By fostering collaboration in the Cosmic Classroom, we can create a learning environment that is supportive, inclusive, and inspiring. This chapter highlights the importance of collaborative learning and invites readers to consider how they can promote collaboration in their own educational practices.

8

Chapter 8: Personalized Learning in the Digital Age

Personalized learning is an approach that tailors education to the individual needs and preferences of each student. In the digital age, technology has made it possible to deliver personalized learning experiences that are more effective and engaging than ever before. In this chapter, we explore the principles of personalized learning and the ways that technology is being used to create customized educational experiences.

One of the key benefits of personalized learning is the ability to address the diverse needs of students. Not all students learn in the same way, and personalized learning allows educators to provide targeted support and resources that meet each student's unique needs. In this chapter, we discuss the various methods and tools that can be used to deliver personalized learning, from adaptive learning platforms to individualized lesson plans. By embracing personalized learning, we can create a more inclusive and equitable educational environment.

Technology plays a crucial role in enabling personalized learning. Digital tools and platforms can collect data on student performance and use algorithms to recommend customized learning pathways. In this chapter, we examine the impact of technology on personalized learning and the ways that it can be used to enhance student engagement and achievement. We also discuss the potential challenges of personalized learning, such as ensuring data privacy and maintaining a balance between technology and human interaction.

Personalized learning also offers the opportunity for students to take ownership of their education. By providing students with choices and allowing them to set their own learning goals, we can empower them to take an active role in their learning journey. In this chapter, we explore the benefits of student-centered learning and the ways that personalized learning can foster a sense of autonomy and motivation. By putting students at the center of the learning process, we can create a more meaningful and engaging educational experience.

Ultimately, personalized learning represents a shift towards a more student-centered approach to education. By leveraging technology and embracing the principles of personalized learning, we can create a learning environment that is tailored to the unique needs and preferences of each student. This chapter highlights the importance of personalized learning in the Cosmic Classroom and invites readers to consider how they can implement personalized learning strategies in their own educational practices.

9

Chapter 9: The Ethics of Educational Technology

As technology becomes increasingly integrated into education, it is essential to consider the ethical implications of its use. In this chapter, we explore the ethical considerations of educational technology, from data privacy to digital equity. By examining the ethical challenges and opportunities, we can ensure that technology is used responsibly and for the benefit of all students.

One of the key ethical considerations is data privacy. Educational technology often involves the collection and analysis of student data, which raises important questions about how this data is used and protected. In this chapter, we discuss the importance of data privacy and the measures that can be taken to safeguard student information. We also examine the potential risks of data breaches and the ways that educators and technology providers can mitigate these risks.

Digital equity is another important ethical consideration. As technology becomes more integral to education, it is essential to ensure that all students have access to the tools and resources they need to succeed. In this chapter, we explore the challenges of digital equity and the ways that educators can work to bridge the digital divide. We discuss the importance of providing access to technology and the role of policy and advocacy in promoting digital equity.

The ethical use of technology also involves considering the impact of technology on student well-being. While technology can offer many benefits, it can also contribute to issues such as screen fatigue, cyberbullying, and social isolation. In this chapter, we examine the potential negative effects of technology and the ways that educators can promote healthy and balanced technology use. We discuss the importance of fostering digital citizenship and the role of educators in guiding students to use technology responsibly.

Ultimately, the ethical considerations of educational technology are complex and multifaceted. By engaging with these ethical challenges, we can ensure that technology is used in ways that are responsible, inclusive, and beneficial for all students. This chapter highlights the importance of ethical considerations in the Cosmic Classroom and invites readers to reflect on the ethical dimensions of their own use of educational technology.

10

Chapter 10: The Future of Learning

The future of learning is an exciting and ever-evolving landscape, shaped by advancements in technology and shifts in educational philosophy. In this chapter, we explore the trends and innovations that are shaping the future of learning, from artificial intelligence to lifelong learning. By considering the possibilities, we can imagine a future where education is more accessible, engaging, and relevant than ever before.

Artificial intelligence (AI) is one of the most significant trends shaping the future of learning. AI has the potential to transform education by providing personalized learning experiences, automating administrative tasks, and offering new tools for assessment and feedback. In this chapter, we examine the ways that AI is being used in education and the potential benefits and challenges of this technology. We discuss the importance of ethical considerations and the role of educators in guiding the responsible use of AI in the classroom.

Lifelong learning is another important trend shaping the future of education. As the pace of technological change accelerates, the need for continuous learning and skill development becomes increasingly important. In this chapter, we explore the concept of lifelong learning and the ways that educational institutions and employers can support ongoing learning and development. We discuss the importance of creating a culture of learning and the role of technology in facilitating lifelong learning opportunities.

The future of learning is also characterized by a shift towards more student-centered and experiential approaches to education. In this chapter, we explore the trends towards project-based learning, experiential learning, and competency-based education. By focusing on real-world applications and hands-on experiences, we can create learning experiences that are more relevant and engaging for students. We discuss the potential benefits and challenges of these approaches and the ways that educators can implement them in their own practices.

Ultimately, the future of learning is about embracing change and innovation to create a more inclusive, engaging, and effective educational experience. By staying informed about the trends and advancements shaping education, we can prepare for the future and ensure that all students have the opportunity to succeed in the Cosmic Classroom. This chapter invites readers to consider the possibilities and reflect on their own vision for the future of learning.

11

Chapter 11: The Search for Meaning

The Cosmic Classroom is not just about acquiring knowledge; it is also about the search for meaning.

In this chapter, we explore the ways that education can help students find purpose and meaning in their lives. By fostering curiosity, encouraging self-reflection, and promoting a sense of connectedness, the Cosmic Classroom becomes a space where students can embark on a journey of self-discovery and personal growth.

Curiosity is a fundamental driver of the search for meaning. When we are curious, we are motivated to explore, ask questions, and seek out new experiences. In this chapter, we discuss the importance of nurturing curiosity in the classroom and the ways that educators can create a learning environment that encourages inquisitiveness. By fostering a culture of curiosity, we can help students develop a lifelong love of learning and a deeper understanding of themselves and the world around them.

Self-reflection is another important aspect of the search for meaning. Through self-reflection, students can examine their own thoughts, feelings, and experiences, gaining insights into their values and goals. In this chapter, we explore the role of self-reflection in education and the various methods that can be used to promote introspection, such as journaling, mindfulness, and discussion. By encouraging self-reflection, we can help students develop a sense of purpose and direction in their lives.

The sense of connectedness is also essential to finding meaning. When students feel connected to their peers, their community, and the broader world, they are more likely to feel a sense of belonging and purpose. In this chapter, we examine the ways that education can promote connectedness, from collaborative projects to community service. By fostering connections, we can help students develop a sense of empathy, responsibility, and civic engagement.

Ultimately, the search for meaning is a deeply personal and ongoing journey. By creating a supportive and nurturing educational environment, we can help students navigate this journey and discover their own unique paths. This chapter highlights the importance of meaning in the Cosmic Classroom and invites readers to reflect on their own search for purpose and fulfillment.

12

Chapter 12: Embracing the Infinite Possibilities

The Cosmic Classroom is a testament to the boundless possibilities of education. As we look to the future, it is essential to embrace the potential of new technologies, innovative methods, and diverse perspectives. In this final chapter, we celebrate the infinite possibilities of the Cosmic Classroom and the ways that we can continue to push the boundaries of learning.

One of the most exciting aspects of the Cosmic Classroom is the opportunity to explore new frontiers of knowledge. From advancements in artificial intelligence to discoveries in space exploration, the possibilities for learning are endless. In this chapter, we discuss the importance of staying curious and open-minded, embracing the unknown, and continuously seeking out new experiences and challenges. By cultivating a sense of wonder and exploration, we can inspire students to pursue their passions and make meaningful contributions to the world.

Innovation is also a key driver of the Cosmic Classroom. By embracing new technologies and methods, we can create more engaging, effective, and inclusive educational experiences. In this chapter, we explore the role of innovation in education and the ways that educators can foster a culture of creativity and experimentation. We discuss the importance of staying informed about emerging trends and being willing to take risks and try new approaches. By nurturing a spirit of innovation, we can ensure that the Cosmic Classroom remains dynamic and relevant.

Diversity is another essential component of the Cosmic Classroom. By celebrating diverse perspectives and experiences, we can create a more inclusive and equitable educational environment. In this chapter, we examine the importance of diversity in education and the ways that educators can promote inclusivity and cultural awareness. We discuss the benefits of diverse narratives, collaborative learning, and student-centered approaches. By embracing diversity, we can enrich the learning experience and help students develop a deeper understanding of themselves and the world.

Ultimately, the Cosmic Classroom represents the infinite possibilities of learning. By embracing curiosity, innovation, and diversity, we can create an educational environment that is truly transformative. This final chapter invites readers to continue exploring the boundless opportunities of the Cosmic Classroom and to join us in the ongoing journey of discovery and growth.

13

Chapter 13: Gamification Beyond the Classroom

While gaming and education have seen a productive intersection within traditional classroom settings, the potential for gamification extends far beyond. This chapter explores the various applications of gamification in different sectors such as corporate training, personal development, and community engagement. By understanding these broader applications, we can see how the principles of game design can be leveraged to enhance learning and motivation in various aspects of life.

In the corporate world, gamification is being used to train employees, foster teamwork, and improve job satisfaction. By incorporating game elements such as point systems, leaderboards, and interactive challenges, companies are creating more engaging and effective training programs. This chapter examines case studies from different industries, highlighting the benefits of gamification in the workplace. We also discuss the challenges and considerations in implementing gamification for professional development.

Personal development is another area where gamification has shown promise. From fitness apps to language learning platforms, game-like elements are being used to motivate individuals to achieve their personal goals. In this chapter, we explore how gamification can support self-improvement by providing structure, feedback, and incentives. We discuss the psychological principles behind gamification and the ways that individuals can use these strategies to stay motivated and on track.

Community engagement is also benefiting from the application of gamification. Nonprofit organizations, government agencies, and social enterprises are using game design principles to engage citizens and promote positive social change. This chapter highlights examples of gamification in action, such as apps that encourage environmental conservation, civic participation, and public health initiatives. By gamifying social good, we can inspire individuals to contribute to their communities and make a meaningful impact.

Ultimately, the principles of gamification can be applied in countless ways to enhance learning and motivation. By exploring these broader applications, we gain a deeper understanding of the potential of gamification to transform various aspects of life. This chapter invites readers to think creatively about how they can incorporate game design principles into their own practices, whether in education, work, or personal development.

14

Chapter 14: Cultivating a Growth Mindset

A growth mindset, the belief that abilities and intelligence can be developed through dedication and hard work, is a powerful concept that can transform the learning experience. In this chapter, we explore the importance of cultivating a growth mindset in the Cosmic Classroom and the ways that gaming and technology can support this mindset.

One of the key components of a growth mindset is the willingness to embrace challenges and learn from failures. In a game, failure is not seen as an endpoint but as an opportunity to try again and improve. This chapter examines how gaming can help students develop resilience and persistence, encouraging them to view challenges as opportunities for growth. By creating a learning environment that supports a growth mindset, we can help students develop the confidence and motivation they need to succeed.

Feedback is another crucial element of a growth mindset. In the Cosmic Classroom, games and technology provide immediate and actionable feedback, helping students understand their progress and identify areas for improvement. In this chapter, we discuss the role of feedback in fostering a growth mindset and the ways that educators can provide constructive feedback that supports student development. By emphasizing the process of learning rather than just the outcomes, we can help students develop a more positive and productive approach to their education.

A growth mindset also involves a focus on effort and practice. In the Cosmic Classroom, games and technology can provide opportunities for students to practice their skills and receive recognition for their efforts. In this chapter, we explore how gamified learning environments can motivate students to put in the effort and practice needed to achieve mastery. We discuss the importance of setting realistic and achievable goals and the ways that educators can support students in their journey towards continuous improvement.

Ultimately, cultivating a growth mindset is about fostering a love of learning and a belief in the potential for growth. By embracing the principles of a growth mindset, we can create a learning environment that is both challenging and supportive. This chapter highlights the importance of a growth mindset in the Cosmic Classroom and invites readers to consider how they can promote this mindset in their own educational practices.

15

Chapter 15: The Power of Reflection

Reflection is a powerful tool for learning and growth, allowing students to make connections between their experiences and their understanding of the material. In this final chapter, we explore the importance of reflection in the Cosmic Classroom and the ways that gaming and technology can facilitate reflective practices.

Reflective practices help students develop a deeper understanding of their learning experiences. By taking the time to reflect on what they have learned, students can identify their strengths, recognize areas for improvement, and make meaningful connections between different concepts. This chapter examines the various methods of reflection, from journaling to discussions, and the ways that educators can incorporate these practices into the classroom. By encouraging reflection, we can help students develop critical thinking skills and a more comprehensive understanding of the material.

Gaming offers unique opportunities for reflection, as players can analyze their strategies, decisions, and outcomes. In this chapter, we explore how games can be used to promote reflective thinking, encouraging students to consider the impact of their choices and learn from their experiences. We discuss the importance of providing opportunities for students to debrief and reflect on their gaming experiences, and the ways that educators can facilitate these discussions.

Technology also plays a crucial role in supporting reflective practices. Digital tools can provide platforms for students to record and share their reflections, receive feedback, and track their progress over time. In this chapter, we examine the ways that technology can enhance reflection, from online journals to digital portfolios. By leveraging technology, we can create a more interactive and dynamic reflective process that supports student growth and development.

Ultimately, reflection is an essential component of the learning journey. By creating a learning environment that values and supports reflection, we can help students develop a deeper understanding of themselves and their learning experiences. This final chapter highlights the power of reflection in the Cosmic Classroom and invites readers to embrace reflective practices in their own educational endeavors.

The Classroom of the Cosmos: Gaming, Learning, and the Search for Meaning

In a world where traditional education often falls short of engaging students, "The Classroom of the Cosmos" explores the limitless possibilities of learning through innovative technologies and unconventional methods. This enlightening book delves into the integration of gaming, virtual reality, and personalized learning to create a Cosmic Classroom that transcends the boundaries of conventional education.

With 15 captivating chapters, readers will journey through the transformative power of gaming as an educational tool, the science of play, the immersive experiences offered by virtual reality, and the profound impact of storytelling. Each chapter offers insights into how these methods can foster a love for learning, promote collaboration, and help students discover their own unique paths to purpose and fulfillment.

The book also addresses the ethical considerations of educational technology, the importance of cultivating a growth mindset, and the role of reflection in the learning process. Through real-world examples, case studies, and thought-provoking discussions, "The Classroom of the Cosmos" invites educators, students, and lifelong learners to reimagine the future of education and embrace the infinite possibilities that lie ahead.

CHAPTER 15: THE POWER OF REFLECTION

Whether you're an educator seeking to inspire your students, a parent looking to support your child's learning journey, or a curious reader eager to explore the intersection of gaming and education, this book offers a compelling and insightful guide to the evolving landscape of learning.

www.ingramcontent.com/pod-product-compliance
Lightning Source LLC
LaVergne TN
LVHW020502080526
838202LV00057B/6118